The Courageous and Self-Respecting Gift of Saying Goodbye

For anyone considering parting ways in a relationship and who needs the strength to let go

Patricia Clare Gallagher BA, MBA

Copyright © 2015 Patricia C. Gallagher

All rights reserved. No part of this book may be reproduced in any form without permission except by a reviewer who may quote brief passages in a review. For permission, please contact the author. Patricia Gallagher welcomes interviews, consultations and speaking engagements.

Patricia C. Gallagher BA, MBA
Box 561
Worcester, PA 19490
Phone: 267-939-0365
www.patriciausa.com

Library of Congress Cataloging-in-Publication Data Pending
Patricia Gallagher 1951
The courageous and self-respecting gift of saying Goodbye - for anyone considering parting ways in a relationship and who needs the strength to let go/ Patricia Gallagher

ISBN-978-1512020434

Disclaimer:

The information in this book is not meant to convey medical or professional advice. Please seek professional care in all matters related to physical or emotional concerns. The author of the book does not prescribe treatment or advice – directly or indirectly. The information provided is the personal opinion of the author. The intent is to provide content of a general nature. The author is not engaged in rendering medical, psychological, emotional, mental or physical advice. The book is not a substitute for seeking competent medical, legal and psychological advice.

Dedication:

To my beautiful family:

John, Robin, Katelyn, Kristen and Ryan

I said to the man who stood at the gate of the year, "Give me a light that I may tread safely into the unknown." And he said, "Go out into the darkness and put thine hand into the hand of God. This will be to thee better than a light and safer than a known way."

The Gate of the Year

Minnie Louise Haskins

(1875-1957)

INTRODUCTION
IS HE GOOD ENOUGH FOR YOU?

Sometimes you have to leave a relationship, even when you love or care for someone very much. Red flags have popped up and you have minimized them or tried to ignore them.

I have counseled women in transition for many years. There were lots of women who stayed in bad relationships for way too long. They shared their thoughts, heartaches and experiences with me. The tips in this book have been gleaned from their experiences. I have put them into this book as a "wake-up call" for young women, older women and those in between.

Do you find yourself worrying, obsessing, and trying so hard to work things out? Have you given your best to have someone understand why you feel hurt, disappointed, sad or frustrated? Have you

had the same discussion over and over again with the same results?

You spoke honestly - from your heart. Unfortunately, there is some sort of a disconnect, and then a time comes when you say, "I deserve better." Maybe something happened. Maybe you heard something or saw something that told you that the time to end the relationship is now. It is time to disembark from the crazy train.

You have decided that *enough is enough* - that you are tired of being upset, disrespected or disappointed. It is hard. It is sad. You may wonder if you are making the right decision.

Remember what you know, what your heart knows, what your head knows. You know what you know! You must trust what you know.

Sadly, someone may have broken your heart and said Goodbye to you. They may have told you *I am out of here, I am leaving, I don't love you, I love you as a friend, I don't care for*

you, I don't like you anymore, It is time for us to part ways, I am not a 24/7 type of guy, I am not over my ex-relationship, I have met someone else or *I never loved you*. It may be a distance thing, an "I do not want to commit" thing, an addiction thing or "I'm just not that into you" thing. It is understandably difficult. It takes courage to accept such harsh words. He is not for you!

We have all been there. But in many cases, that is what you must do - give yourself the Gift of Acceptance followed by giving yourself *The Courageous and Self-Respecting Gift of Saying Goodbye* - and the gift for you will be The Gift of Self-Respect.

You cannot change someone. The issues that someone has with you and others have been with that person a long time - long before you came along. It will be a gift for you to move on. Think of it not as *rejection* but as *redirection. And it is protection.*

You are giving yourself a gift by saying Goodbye to someone who does not want to

be with you, does not have time for you, makes excuses not to be with you, has used you, has lied to you, has lied by omission to you, has hurt you, has disappointed you, has frustrated you, has confused you, or who is just plain old unhealthy for you.

The encouraging thoughts provided in **The Courageous and Self-Respecting Gift of Saying Goodbye** may apply to your situation. You can start at the beginning or open to a random page. The reflections may be a reminder that you deserve more than someone who is not treating you in a respectful, kind, thoughtful, honest and unselfish way.

Take good care of yourself. You can do it! You are not alone. Many others have taken this path before you. I wish you peace and joy, today and always.

Patricia Gallagher

PEOPLE COME INTO YOUR LIFE FOR A REASON, A SEASON, OR A LIFETIME

People come into your life for a reason, a season, or a lifetime. When you figure out which one it is, you will know what to do for each person. When someone is in your life for a "reason," it is usually to meet a need you have expressed. They have come to assist you at a difficult time, to provide you with guidance and support, and to aid you physically, emotionally, or spiritually. They may seem like a godsend, and they are! They are there for the reason you need them to be. Then, without any wrong doing on your part, or at an inconvenient time, this person will say or do something to bring the relationship to an end. Sometimes they die. Sometimes they walk away. Sometimes they act up and force you to take a stand. What we must realize is that our need has been met, our desire has been fulfilled, and his work is done. The

prayer you sent up has been answered. And now it is time to move on.

    When people come into your life for a "season," it is because your turn has come to share, grow, or learn. They bring you an experience of peace or make you laugh. They may teach you something you have never done. They usually give you an unbelievable amount of joy. Believe it! It is real – but, only for a season.

    "Lifetime" relationships teach lifetime lessons; these are things you must build upon in order to have a solid emotional foundation. Your job is to accept the lesson, love the person, and put what you have learned to use in all other areas of your life. (Anonymous)

LET HIM GO!

Is there someone in your romantic life that is trying to walk away from the relationship? Is he playing games with you? On again and off again? Making you sad? Making you cry? Making you miserable? Let him go! If you have to try to talk someone into coming to your house, calling you, being with you or doing a simple favor for you – let him go. Save your self-respect and dignity as a woman of valor and value. I have this saying in a frame near my desk.

You are a ruby, a diamond and gold combined. Who can find a virtuous woman? For the price is far above rubies; strength and honor are her clothing.

You cannot make anyone stay with you. You do not want to lower yourself to beg, talk into or manipulate someone to be your boyfriend, partner or significant other. You know when the fire is out. You know when it is getting to be too much trouble for you.

You know when something is just not right. Something is fishy. Something inside of you is telling you critical information about the truth of your relationship. Stop trying to talk someone into doing anything. It is not going to work. Trying to change someone else is like trying to shovel smoke! Remember: If God wants someone in your life, He will make a way for that to happen. God is protecting you now. God is re-directing you now! Listen to His message. It is for your highest good.

LETTERS FROM WOMEN WHO SAID GOODBYE

Dear Patricia,

I had a wonderful man involved in my life for the past three years. But Prince Charming fell off his white horse. It was so subtle. The things that I had an inkling about became very clear towards the end. I had to give myself The Gift of Saying Goodbye. Honestly, there is still a void where he was. I want to be with someone that I can count on to go to the ends of the earth for me. And I want to do the same for him. I am glad that I had the courage to say I AM DONE. But it was hard. He had different expectations about what a relationship should be. He was not a "giver" - only when it was convenient for him. Thank you for helping me to see the situation as it truly was. Nancy

Dear Patricia,

You confirmed what I was feeling. I heard you being interviewed on a radio show. Your words clarified what was going in my relationship. Thank you for helping me process my thoughts. His idea of a relationship is with a six pack of beer and a sporting event, night after night. He just never makes me a priority. Time to let him go. Time to say Goodbye.

Karen

INSPIRATION, GUIDANCE, WISDOM, TIPS, HOPE, OBSERVATIONS, SUGGESTIONS, GEMS, REMINDERS

 1. When you feel that your self-esteem is being chipped away or diminished by personal criticism, speak right up. Speak up even if it feels like the words are getting caught in your throat.

 2. If someone does not value you for the person that you are, you do not need them in your life.

3. If someone brings up things from the past over and over again in an effort to shame you, make you feel guilty, trap you, intimidate you, or make you defensive or uncomfortable, it is time to trust your intuition and say Goodbye. Things will not get better.

4. If your partner asks you questions about your past relationships or former life but is not open when you ask things about his past, there is something "fishy" going on. Your inner guide will tell you when something is

not right.

⭐ 5. God, please tell me what I need to know about this relationship.

⭐ 6. It is okay to say NO. No is a complete sentence. There is great value and personal power in saying NO.

⭐ 7. Think about giving yourself The Courageous and Self-Respecting Gift of Saying Goodbye when you are sick and tired of being sick and tired.

8. You can set limits and still be a good person.

9. Think about giving yourself The Courageous and Self-Respecting Gift of Saying Goodbye when you are tired of being let down, lied to, and disappointed.

10. You have turned a blind eye to some of his actions and words. Now it is time to see the issues as they really are.

11. Take this new journey – one day at a time.

12. Don't give him a second chance. It is really probably about the third or fourth chance anyway.

13. Thank you, God, for giving me the courage to leave a destructive relationship. Thank you for giving me the strength and wisdom to leave a relationship that was unhealthy for me.

⭐ 14. What don't you trust about this person? What makes you feel fed up? Angry? Relationships are supposed to be happy, free-flowing, fun and easy.

⭐ 15. Problems may come up, but your inner voice tells you the difference between little blips on the relationship radar screen and an important issue - such as an irreconcilable difference.

⭐ 16. If you are in a committed relationship - is he loyal? Is he really where he says he is?

⭐ 17. Do you wonder what he is doing when you are not together? Do you have reasons to doubt his truthfulness or fidelity?

⭐ 18. Is he there for you? When you tell him that you are feeling sad, lonely, depressed and miss him, will he come to comfort you?

19. Does he acknowledge your feelings and understand you? Does he have time for you?

20. Is he manipulative? Does he call you spoiled or self-centered? Do you see those traits in him?

21. When he says that he is not looking for a commitment or a committed relationship, believe him the first time. "I think you are looking for a 24/7 relationship. I am not that guy."

22. Avoid the guy who wants you to come to his place most of the time and wants you to drive to see him, more than he does for you.

23. Something is off balance when he wants to do what he wants to do, and you are afraid or hesitant to ask him to do something that you want to do, for fear he will say no or very begrudgingly and unhappily do it.

24. There is reason to be concerned when you tell little white lies because he

will get mad, get even or get irritated.

⭐ 25. Something is not kosher if you find a pair of designer sunglasses in his car – the kind that a lady would wear – and he says he has no idea where they came from.

⭐ 26. I would not get too close to a man who says, "I am still not over my wife" or a previous relationship.

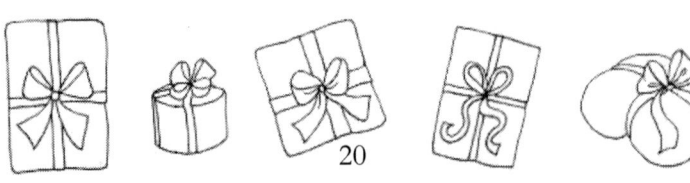

⭐ 27. Does he avoid calling to talk on the phone and insist on doing most of his communicating via text messages?

⭐ 28. Taking on someone's problems that cause you to suffer along with them is not healthy for you. You can have compassion. Be careful of being pulled down into the muck with him.

⭐ 29. Does he turn his cell phone off in his home or leave his cell phone in the car? That's kind of shady.

⭐ 30. Are you afraid of his anger? How does he manifest anger? Has he told you about past anger issues? Has he given you any examples of such issues?

⭐ 31. Have you seen or heard of his road rage?

⭐ 32. Has he pinched, pushed, hit or hurt you in any way? Does he say that he was just playing around? Does he say that you took it the wrong way?

⭐ 33. Has he said that you are too sensitive or prudish? "I don't know of any other woman that would get upset at things like you do."

⭐ 34. He hasn't been faithful in marriage. "I messed around on my wife." Not looking good!

⭐ 35. Has he been in a ton of relationships? Has he not been married in decades? Does he admit he has been called a weasel? When you ask him what went wrong in past relationships, he says,

"I don't know. You would have to ask them." It will probably be more of the same behavior and outcomes with you.

36. The best predictor of future behavior is past behavior.

37. Is he possessive and jealous? The funny thing about men like that is - well, let's just say, from my own experience, they were not being true blue.

⭐ 38. How does it make you feel when he compliments other women in front of you? What about when he openly admires movie stars, models, waitresses, or makes a point to tell you how beautiful his wife was, his former girlfriend, a lady he works with, a neighbor, a friend, etc.? Isn't there a song *I Only Have Eyes for You*?

⭐ 39. Lies of omission are still lies. Little white lies are still lies.

⭐ 40. Will he help you? Will he help your family?

⭐ 41. Is he rigid about his beliefs? "I would never go to your church."

⭐ 42. Your relationship is complicated if you find yourself constantly trying to figure him out. When you are texting, emailing and calling your best friends to talk about your relationship issues - there is trouble brewing. Why would you want to be in a relationship

that takes so much time to try to figure it all out?

43. Does he go with the flow?

44. A bad sign is if he says, "I would never go to a counselor or therapist. They are all crackpots."

45. I feel betrayed. I feel violated. I feel cheated upon. How could you do that to me? I thought our relationship was between just us.

46. He is who he is. Accept that.

47. You are not good enough for me. Not kind enough. Not thoughtful enough. You have nothing to offer me. I must preserve my self-respect and walk away. (This is the message that you tell yourself.)

48. Do not think that an addiction will just pass.

⭐ 49. Are you thriving with this person in your life?

⭐ 50. A person who makes jokes that put people down or are offensive is not the kind of person you want to get tangled up with.

⭐ 51. Stay away from a guy who puts you down, corrects you, tells you what to do or how to do it. How to close windows, lower the window shades, close a car door, put away an iron, butter a bagel, make a bed, etc.

☆ 52. Do you walk on eggshells when you are around him? The tricky part is that he is not always like that. He can be sweet, complimentary and seem like your biggest fan. Don't be fooled by that charm. You have overlooked too many of his character defects.

☆ 53. Do you feel guilty when you say "no" about something? Are you afraid that you will lose him? Do you hesitate to set limits with him? Are you afraid

that he will break up if you make demands of his time?

54. Do you wonder, "What is this relationship? Are we committed? Are we a couple? Or are we just dating?"

55. You may think this relationship is starting to feel crazy. It probably is a little crazy if your intuition is telling you so.

56. Have you written down all of the good, fun and exciting parts of the

relationship? Make a column for the times that you had a stomachache, headache and an emotion-ache - when your feelings were all tangled up inside of you. When this happens more than a few times, your mind, spirit and body are giving clues that he may not be good for you. Let him go - no matter how handsome he is, how good his cologne smells, how you love dancing with him, how you love his hugs and kisses, and how he makes you feel. They are all surface things - not the things of substance that make a relationship work.

⭐ 57. Do you think he might be controlling? You are not sure because you have never experienced a relationship like this one. You might ignore it or minimize it but the issue keeps popping up.

⭐ 58. Is he self-centered and selfish?

⭐ 59. He questions me about things. He doubts some of the things that I tell him.

☆ 60. When a man tells you that you have been spoiled by your ex-husband or a previous relationship, and says that he is not going to put up with your spoiled brat behavior, it is time to evaluate the relationship.

☆ 61. Are you always the one to make amends and say I am sorry? Are you the one that always has to smooth things over? You are not the be-all and end-all of keeping the relationship going.

⭐ 62. Has your partner gone outside of the boundaries of your committed relationship? In any way? You know what I mean.

⭐ 63. Does he deserve you? Is he good enough for you? Kind enough for you? Thoughtful enough for you?

⭐ 64. Does he have, in your opinion, an unhealthy interest in one of your friends? Has he said something inappropriate about her?

⭐ 65. Does he pressure you to do things that make you feel uncomfortable? Romantically or morally?

⭐ 66. Are you embarrassed by things that he says or does? If you were with your family and he did such things, how would you feel?

⭐ 67. Are you hesitant to introduce him to some of your friends? Why?

⭐ 68. What would you do if your best friend told you that he is not for

you? That there is just "something" about him. Upon reflection, you admit to yourself that sometimes you get the feeling that he might be "creepy."

69. Has he impacted your mood in negative ways?

70. What is happening when you tell a family member about a serious relationship issue and you try to soften the situation? "But we really DO love/care for each other. He is

really a nice guy." And your relative responds by saying, "There are a lot of other really nice guys." And your best friend tells you that he is not a NICE guy.

71. Is he the kind of man that wants to have his cake and eat it too? You know what that means. You are not the type of woman who has to put up with that nonsense.

72. Are you troubled by his drinking, using drugs, gambling or other

addictions that have manifested in your relationship? The addiction affects the behavior of the person who uses but it also affects you.

73. Make a decision to leave an unhealthy relationship if it is not good for you. This type of situation requires a safe and supportive environment or network of friends to help you stay strong.

74. Go to a therapist to help you sort through your issues. Why am I

attracted to this type of guy? What do I need to change about myself so that this does not happen again? What made me fall for him? Why did I stay this long?

75. Why do I put up with temper tantrums, unacceptable behavior, "shady" things, jealousy, and abusive language? So many things that I cannot figure out about him.

76. It feels good to talk about problems with someone trained to help. You

need understanding, support and a strategy to cope. Don't blame yourself.

77. Don't keep the relationship problems a secret. Confide in a trusted friend or two. Each time that you share part of the story, you will see the problem more clearly. You are not looking for sympathy but understanding and feedback.

78. Talk to yourself. Listen to yourself. As you drive in your car, talk aloud

about what is going on in your mind. You will come to realize that the person has a negative effect on you.

79. Are you running on empty? It is time to fill your love tank! Today is the first day for you to start caring for yourself.

80. Healthy attracts healthy. When you are emotionally healthy, you will not put up with someone who is not a healthy communicator and problem

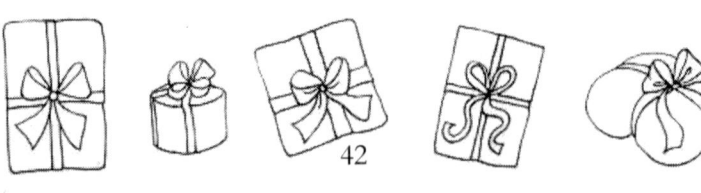

solver.

81. He is not who you thought he was. He has a dark side. He has put his best foot forward. Now the walls are cracking. You are seeing a man who is not good for you. It may be hard. It will be hard. But staying with him would be much harder. Bail out now!

82. Think about the following words. How do the words relate to your relationship? Worry, money

problems, cancels plans, lies, upset, makes threats, gives ultimatums, afraid to upset him, hurt, embarrassed, fear, anxiety, feel like a failure, ashamed, need help, furious, denial, nervous, anguish, chaos, morality.

83. Don't put more effort into making the relationship work than your partner does. Of course, you must continue to work on your own issues. Work on yourself so that you are emotionally healthy. Do not try too hard to

make things perfect for someone who is not doing the same for you or for someone who is not that invested in you.

84. Has anybody ever warned you about him? Someone in his family say anything? "He was really mean when I was growing up."

85. I didn't cause his problems. I cannot cure his problems. I cannot control his problems.

86. It is futile to try to fix someone else. Trying to change someone else is like going to the hardware store for milk.

87. Does he punish you or get back at you? You are not alone. That is a sign of a dysfunctional and emotionally abusive relationship.

88. Read up or Google the topic of mental, emotional, verbal and physical abuse. You will find lots of articles

written by people who honestly share their struggles to help others.

89. Denial is a means of refusing to accept how serious of a problem you have on your hands.

90. Are you confused and conflicted about what to do? Should I leave the relationship? How? Will I regret it if I leave him?

91. You might think that if you are prettier, more interesting, more (anything) ...that he will treat you

better and be more faithful and attentive. Not true!

92. Make changes that you want to make for yourself. Maybe you want to look your best. Engage in new hobbies or interests if that is what YOU want to do. "You should wear your hair up. You should not wear glasses. You would look better with longer hair." "Don't wear that make-up." Focus on yourself for a change.

93. The more you listen, the more you learn. Listen to personal growth radio and internet shows. Read books. Learn what you can about emotional pain, fears, insecurities, failing at things, standing up for yourself, speaking your truth and finding solutions. You will find a lot of information about troubled relationships and how to get off the merry-go-round of denial, desperation and sadness.

94. You have so many gifts within you. He is not your strength. You have strength within yourself. Do not let

yourself be pulled into the "Poor me, how will I ever get along without him?" syndrome.

95. Think of some of the negative events that occurred recently. If you are honest, your relationship was not all that happy. Things have been adding up. Building up inside of you. You did not want to see them. You were not sure about what you suspected. You did not have proof until now. Then, you knew that you could no longer minimize or deny the red flags.

96. Change how you behave. You do not have to accept unacceptable behavior. Make a plan to move forward in your life.

97. I know that you think you love him. Or really cared about him. You thought that your relationship had a good chance of making it. Did you contort your face at times and wonder, "Why would he say that to me? Why would he even think that about me?" I am not that kind of

woman and he knows that. Think about the whole package. He might not be a box of chocolates after all!

98. The pain that you experience disengaging from someone who is not good for you will enable you to help someone else. Say thank you to God for the blessing of the relationship and for what you learned about yourself. Thank God also for the blessing of leaving the relationship when it was no longer kind, nurturing, gentle and respectful. Say

Goodbye to fear, resentment, confusion, hurt, and disappointment. Say hello to the new confidence in yourself and growth in self-esteem.

99. It may be scary. It will take work but you can do it. Be easy on yourself. Calmly sort out "your own stuff." You won't know how strong you really are until you stand alone.

100. We all make mistakes. We all act inappropriately at times. We all

choose relationships that may not be what we initially thought.

⭐ 101. Forgive yourself for being human and change what you can.

⭐ 102. It probably actually shocks you when you tell a trusted friend of an incident that happened with your partner. An incident that you know was way out of line in a supposedly caring relationship.

⭐ 103. Make amends to anyone that you have hurt with your words and actions.

⭐ 104. Forgive yourself for what you did when you were in pain or were lonely.

⭐ 105. In this relationship, you settled for someone beneath your standards in many ways.

⭐ 106. You needed him for a season of your life……he does not deserve a woman as wonderful as you are.

⭐ 107. He has duped a lot of people such as the friends who think that he is Mr. Wonderful. That is what you thought for a time too. He is not all bad. Honestly, there were so many things that were wonderful, fun and exciting. It is a shame that he had to "wreck it" by acting in ways that were unacceptable for you.

108. Has he ever told you to "Shut up? Shut your mouth. Can you just shut up? You can't keep anything quiet. You have such a big mouth."

109. Has he cursed at you? Has he left you stranded anywhere? Have you told him that you wanted to go home and he refused to drive you back?

110. "Clean up your side of the street."

111. I think it is important to say this. Leaving a relationship when you still

care, still love, and are afraid to really cut the ties, is difficult to do. You have to maintain your leverage as woman who is strong and wise. You know that there are things about the relationship that would always be a problem. He is not going to change that much for you. You either have to accept him as he is....totally ....or move on.

112. Just think of how horrible you feel when there is tension between you. Notice how you wait for him to say

something that will make things better and he won't. How you have the same argument/discussion over and over again. "Insanity is doing the same thing over and over again expecting different results." Or as Dr. Phil would say, "How's that working for you?"

113. Are you happy? You deserve trust, kindness, love, attention, respect and affection. Don't settle for less than the right person for you!

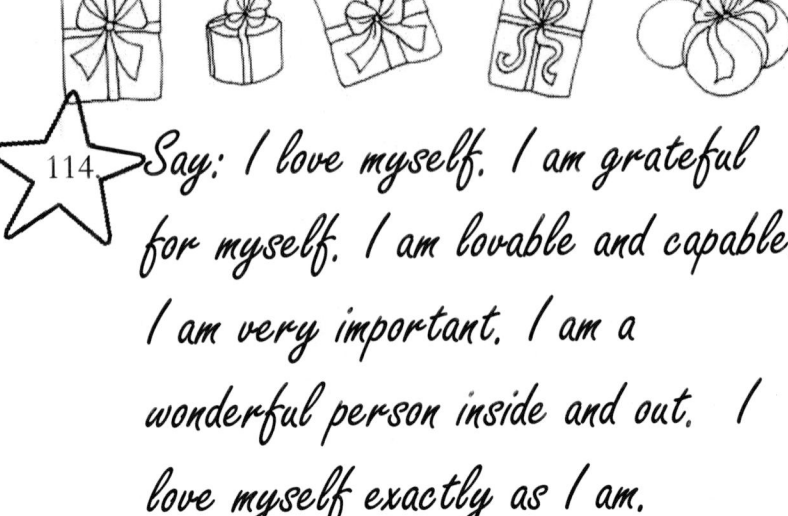

114. Say: I love myself. I am grateful for myself. I am lovable and capable. I am very important. I am a wonderful person inside and out. I love myself exactly as I am.

115. It is time to put on a new pair of clean glasses so that you can see things as they really are. Maybe for the first time, you will realize that he is not the man that you thought he was.

⭐ 116. Sometimes you have to leave a relationship. Even when you love or care for someone very much. Red flags have popped up and you have minimized them or tried to ignore them.

⭐ 117. You find yourself worrying, obsessing, and trying so hard to work things out. Giving your best to have him understand why you feel hurt, disappointed, sad or frustrated. Is it futile?

118. You have the same discussion over and over again. You speak from your heart. Then a time comes when you say to yourself, "I deserve better." Maybe something happens.

119. Does he give you the silent treatment?

120. Does he not return your call or text?

121. Have you seen inappropriate things on his phone or computer?

122. Maybe you heard something or saw something that told you that the time is now. The time to disembark from the crazy train. That enough is enough!

123. It is hard. It is sad. You may wonder if it is the right decision. It is at that time that you should remember what you know - what your heart knows. What your head knows.

☆ 124. In many cases, here is what you must do - give yourself the Gift of Acceptance. You cannot change him.

☆ 125. Or, what if someone has broken your heart and said Goodbye to you? Told you that he is leaving, doesn't love you or care for you or even like you anymore. Or he is attracted to someone else. Believe me, it is a gift to know that. You do not want to be with someone like that.

126. *"A woman that I used to date, a pretty lady, called and asked me to go to lunch. I just want to go as a friend. I don't like her anymore or anything like that. What should I tell her? How do you feel about that? Would you be upset with me if I went?"*

127. It may be a distance thing, an *"I do not want to commit"* thing, an *"I just don't feel like doing that with you"* thing, an addiction thing or *"I'm just not that into you"* thing. You don't

need a THING with that kind of guy.

⭐ 128. It is understandably difficult. It takes courage to accept his harsh words. Sometimes you are so shocked by his words that you do not know how to respond. So you remain silent. But you remember.

⭐ 129. We have all been there. You may have heard that hurt people hurt people. He may be hurt or wounded by life. There are trained

professionals available to help him. You can be there to support him but not carry him. The burden is too much for you.

130. Do you ever wonder why the person that you feel closest to hurts you the most?

131. "I would never do that to him."

132. Some guys have anxiety. What does he do to calm his anxiety? What

addiction does he engage in? That is a temporary fix.

133. And all addictions shut you out. The addiction is his mistress. It is his secret life. There are so many parts of his life that you do not know about. He has a "parallel universe" going on – that does not involve you.

134. Dr. Phil says that for every lie you know about, there are a ton that you do not know about.

⭐ 135. Dr. Phil has said on his show that addicts lie. That is just what they do. It is part of the disease. They cannot let you in on that secret life.

⭐ 136. Begin your new life. Start looking for all of the glorious things in life. Repeat to yourself: I am going to live my life gloriously!

⭐ 137. Have you ever thought that your partner is an "oddball?"

138. Have you put up with more than your fair share of broken promises and unmet expectations?

139. Don't waste your time with someone who does not know what/who they want. Is he waffling back and forth between interest in you and another love interest? Respect yourself enough to walk away.

140. The issues that he has with you and others have been with him a long time. Long before you came along. It

will be a gift to you to move on. Astonishing but so true.

141. Your trust was eroded. You felt bad. You didn't think he was that type of man.

142. Have you noticed him flirting? Yes, in a way that clearly tells someone else that he is interested. It is not that you are jealous. You are concerned about your relationship. Protecting what you have.

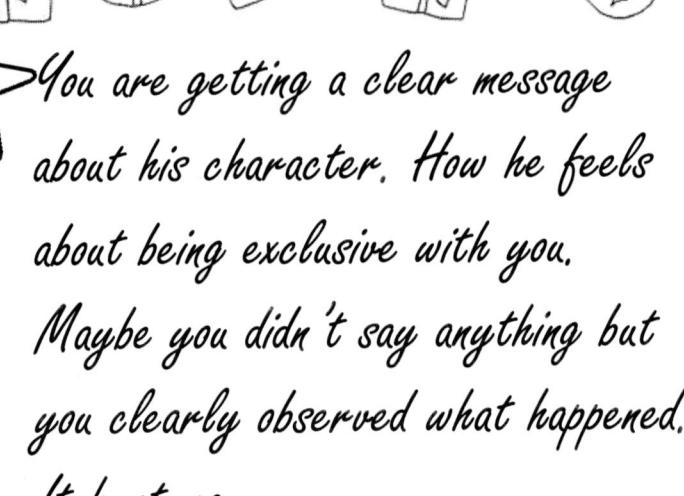

★ 143. You are getting a clear message about his character. How he feels about being exclusive with you. Maybe you didn't say anything but you clearly observed what happened. It hurt you.

★ 144. Or maybe you did think or suspected that he was not a One Woman Man although that is the way that he presented himself. Now you have more information.

☆ 145. You are giving yourself a gift by saying Goodbye to someone who does not want to be with you.

☆ 146. Think about the words in The Courageous and Self-Respecting Gift of Goodbye reflections. Take good care of yourself. Extremely good care.

☆ 147. Learn from the experiences of others.

148. Does he lash out at the dog, co-workers, people at the gym, and drivers on the road, family members, or a former partner? Do you see a pattern here? Do not allow him any justification for hurting other people.

149. Do you feel sad and sorry for yourself? Don't you want to be happy again? Peaceful inside? Reflect on what is causing the tension in your life. Don't go back.

⭐ 150. Give yourself the gift of "It's Moving Day"- the moment when you know that you cannot do this anymore. Decide that you are going to move on.

⭐ 151. Don't go back to old patterns of accepting what is not respectful. You know what you are feeling. Your feelings are valid. Think of the strongest woman in your circle of friends. How would she handle this situation?

152. God, grant me the eyes to see what You want me to see, ears to hear what is important for me to hear, legs to walk where you want me to go, a mouth to say what needs to be said and the courage to make decisions that are right for me. Give me the strength to walk away from things that are uncomfortable, just plain wrong for me, unacceptable and out of balance.

153. Is your relationship one of cooperation and teamwork? Are you learning, growing and maturing together? If

not, think about letting go. Letting him go.

154. Are there things that you have wanted to do and have put off because he does not want to do them with you? Have you wanted to travel and he does not want to? Have you wanted to take dance lessons and he does not want to? Have you wanted to get together with other couples for dinner and he does not want to? Have you wanted him to spend more time with your family? Yes, you can do these things alone. But if you

personally want to do "couple things" and he does not want to....well, sometimes in a healthy relationship, you do things anyway to make your partner happy.

155. Are you enabling some of his behaviors by not speaking up? Say what you mean, mean what you say but don't say it mean.

156. Find a quiet place to pray, meditate and write about what you are feeling.

⭐ 157. You may have to take an assertiveness training class or a healthy communication workshop. It is worth it to become an instrument of change. You will have a better future when you learn ways to stand up for what is important to you.

⭐ 158. Does he try to tell you how to handle situations or why you should or should not do things? "You are just bothering people." "Why do you have to talk to everybody that you see?" "I think you are being flirty

with him. I saw the way that you looked at him and you think that I didn't notice." "Why don't you just leave well enough alone?"

159. Don't try to beg him to stay when he says "We are just beating a dead horse talking about all of this stuff over and over again. I think we have reached the end of the road. It is time for us to part, don't you think? We can still be friends with benefits if you want to...."

160. When was the last time that you went to sleep easily, with a smile in your heart, with nothing on your mind and woke up with a feeling of excitement about your life?

161. Do you feel guilty when you say no about something? Are you afraid that you will lose him? Do you hesitate to set limits with him? Are you afraid he will break up with you if you make too many demands of his time?

162. Are you grinding your teeth, biting your lip, experiencing pain in your

neck.....or anything else that indicates that this relationship is causing you great stress?

163. Leaving him now will save you buckets of tears in the future. You don't want to cry tears of sadness and frustration for the rest of your life.

164. Are you always the one to make amends and say I am sorry? Are you the one that always has to smooth things over?

⭐ 165. Trying to change someone is as futile as trying to shovel smoke.

⭐ 166. You do not have to attend every fight that you are invited to.

⭐ 167. It is going to be hard. For weeks. Maybe for months. For a year. You will be tempted to contact him. Don't do it. Maintain your relationship sobriety — one day at a time. Don't relapse by calling him. Then you will be back to square one.

168. Feeling brokenhearted now? It is devastating to have your heart broken. It is hard to really say Goodbye.

169. Remember that you are not a failure because the relationship did not work out. It takes two to tango!

170. Clear all of this "debris" so that you have room for a better person to appear. Someone who loves you

unconditionally. In a healthy and loving way.

171. When you go back over the many situations that seemed a little odd, can you now connect the dots?

172. Are you tired of being disappointed? Want relief? Write down all of your feelings about this relationship – all of them.

173. Don't let another person "rent space" in your head.

174. Do his words match his actions? Do not believe what he says with his mouth. Believe what his actions indicate.

175. Pretend that you hear your father's voice telling him that he has worn out his welcome and to get lost. Get really lost.

176. Trust the process of letting go.

177. Reclaim your spirit! Nurture the person within.

178. There is a very heavy price to pay when you stay in an unhealthy relationship.

179. Clear the emotional wreckage from your life. Bulldoze it. Dynamite it. Get rid of the heartache, misery, frustration and confusion.

⭐ 180. You are not alone.

⭐ 181. Give yourself a day to be alone. Get comfortable on your couch. Sit in a church. Do both. Cry. Think. Pray. Listen to peaceful music. Listen to hymns of comfort. The kind that tell you to "Be not afraid." You may feel depressed. There might be a lump in your throat. Hurt in your heart. You are probably wondering what he is thinking. What are you thinking? That you are tired of being hurt by his behavior. Ask God to give you

the words to say. To show you the next step to take.

⭐ 182. God, please help me. This is so hard because I still have feelings for him despite all that I know now.

⭐ 183. Sadness? Loneliness? Depression? Is that what you are experiencing now?

⭐ 184. Staying in the relationship would take you down much lower than where you are now.

⭐ 185. Accept yourself.

⭐ 186. Plant seeds for a happier life. Starting right now. Write down the things that you want to do that make you smile. Do them. Do the things that make you happy.

⭐ 187. Detach from unhealthy people.

⭐ 188. Experience is what you get when you do not get what you want.

⭐ 189. There comes a time when you can no longer deny what is happening in the relationship.

⭐ 190. Remain focused. Plan your action.

⭐ 191. Let Go and Let God. Let go of the situations that you cannot control.

⭐ 192. When you are really serious about giving yourself The Courageous and Self-Respecting Gift of Saying Goodbye, have no contact with the

person or anyone else that can give you information about him. Become invisible.

193. Are you obsessing? Lord, let me know something or hear something that will give me clarity about the issue.

194. Do you ever feel that you are in a black hole – emotionally, spiritually or mentally? What is the lesson that the experience of this relationship has taught you?

⭐ 195. Find a healthy way to get your anger and sadness out. Keeping it in is harmful.

⭐ 196. Your relationship probably had times of peace and fun. And times of calamity and crises. You know when the fire is out of control. You know when it can no longer be stomped out. It is hard to leave. You will know when it is time. Your life depends on it. Feel the fear and do it anyway.

197. You can't go in the river without getting wet. To me, that means that you cannot stay in an unhealthy relationship without getting hurt. This relationship is teaching you something.

198. Going through the feelings and emotions will get you to the freedom at the other side.

199. You are powerless over his sneaky behavior and bad choices. You cannot be with him 24 hours a day, checking

on him and monitoring him. Why do you even want to be with someone that you do not trust?

⭐ 200. How often do you feel frightened or confused by someone's out-of-control baggage?

⭐ 201. Post this on your bathroom mirror. I want to live a peaceful and serene life.

⭐ 202. Did you ever feel that there is a monster within the person? Do you have to tame his anger?

203. There is really a big gift for you when you say Goodbye.

204. God has not picked this person for you if there are so many issues in the relationship.

205. Is the person opinionated? Selfish? A poor listener? A blamer?

206. Can you see why this person came into your life at this time?

★ 207. Look at yourself in the mirror? Do you look happy?

★ 208. Learn how to commit to yourself. Save some love for yourself! Go to meetings, take a line dancing class, learn a new language or take a course online or at the local adult evening school.

★ 209. "Belong" to something. It is healing to be a part of some kind of group for support. Let people get to know

you and care for you. Find a sense of comfort by joining a community service organization, tutor at the local elementary school or volunteer to serve food at a shelter.

210. Look for healthy and helpful friends to accompany you on the journey of living your life in a positive way. Hang out with people who are moving forward.

211. Make a commitment to read books with positive messages. Write your

feelings and notes in the margins.

⭐ 212. Don't play the victim. Be strong. You know the reason for the need to break-up. The other person knows what needs to happen and what needs to change for you to stay.

⭐ 213. Let people hug you, help you, and walk with you through this life-changing event.

⭐ 214. I love this saying: "Nothing changed; I changed - and everything changed."

215. Give the outcome to God. God is my adviser.

216. Take control of your life again. Get a fresh start. Move to higher ground. Get out of the dangerous area.

217. Are you tired of hurting? Tired of tears? Tired of pain and uncertainty?

218. Have you observed abnormal behavior in the relationship?

219. Are you looking for love in all of the wrong places?

220. Trust me. It will become apparent why The Courageous and Self-Respecting Gift of Saying Goodbye is a wonderful gift to you. It is an empowerment tool. Your self-esteem will grow. You will eventually see the true blessing.

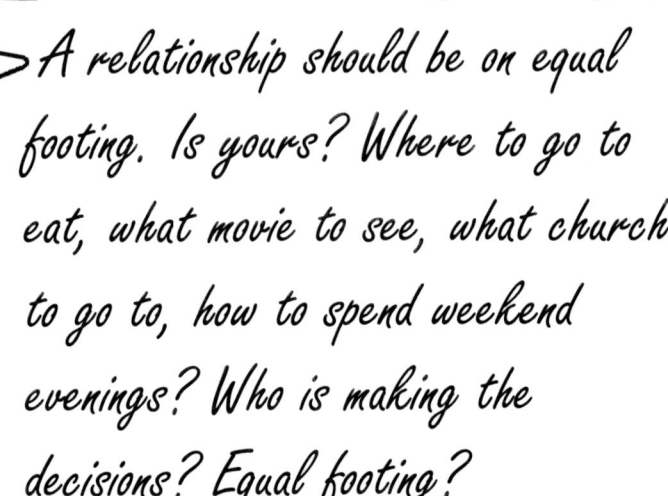

⭐ 221. A relationship should be on equal footing. Is yours? Where to go to eat, what movie to see, what church to go to, how to spend weekend evenings? Who is making the decisions? Equal footing?

⭐ 222. You always have choices. You do not have to wait until you hit rock bottom. You do not want to get to that point. Pick yourself up. Tell yourself that you can do it. Make the change. Don't isolate. Find support.

223. Everything happens for a reason. In time, things will be revealed.

224. Set time to set aside to cry. Get your feelings out.

225. You are not responsible for someone else's happiness.

226. You may not be able to do this right away because you may be too angry or hurt, but at some point, you may be able to ask God to bless his

journey.

227. No one can give you everything that you need to be happy. Happiness is an inside job.

228. When someone pushes your buttons, you don't have to push back.

229. Trying to control someone else's behavior makes you out of control. Stave off bad behaviors by detaching. Be gone!

⭐ 230. Why do you like this person? Why do you stay?

⭐ 231. Some of my favorite sayings: If you always do what you have always done, you will always get what you have always gotten. Insanity is doing the same thing over and over again expecting different results. Trying to change someone else is like going to the hardware store for milk. This too shall pass. When you see trouble, you don't have to engage in it.

⭐ 232. Be emotionally honest with yourself and others. Have you felt out of balance in this relationship?

⭐ 233. Yes, you might grieve parts of the relationship even when you are the one to say Goodbye. Stay strong. Pray for resolve and guidance. No matter what happens, you can go on.

⭐ 234. Find the answers within.

235. A painful break-up can be a catalyst for change. Leaving permits you to let go of the pain.

236. We often use denial as a means of refusing to accept the seriousness of the situation. Denial corners people into accepting unacceptable behavior.

237. Oprah says that every experience is a teacher. Make a character checklist in evaluating your next romantic relationship. I bet you will recognize red flags quickly.

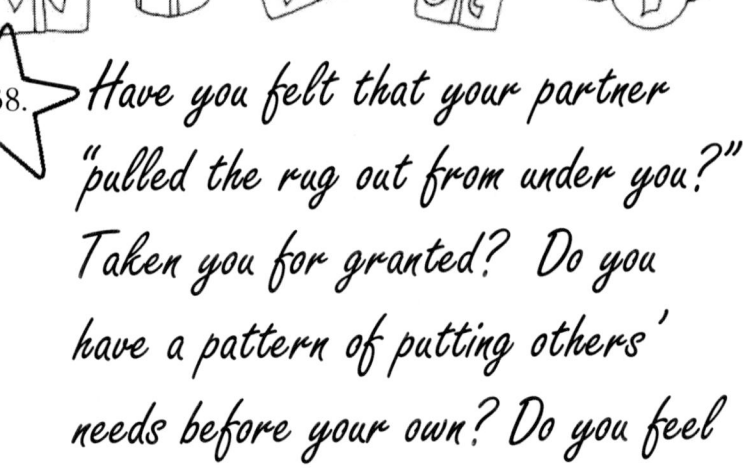

238. Have you felt that your partner "pulled the rug out from under you?" Taken you for granted? Do you have a pattern of putting others' needs before your own? Do you feel resentful?

239. Have you considered that your addiction to a person in an intimate relationship can be as strong and harmful as an addiction to alcohol or drugs?

240. I have to matter first.

241. Respond rather than react. It takes practice but it is effective.

242. The path to peace is accepting people, places and things. Accepting does not mean remaining in the situation. You can use your "right of personal decision" to excuse yourself from anything that is unsafe or unhealthy for your well-being.

243. Are you ashamed or embarrassed by his behavior?

244. You may experience an odd sense of relief when you part ways.

245. Parting ways with sadness, desperation and pain may be the coping mechanisms that will force you to take a stand.

246. Stand firm. You know the consequences of remaining with him.

247. Do you and your partner have different versions of your

relationship?

⭐ 248. Every experience is a lesson or a blessing - or maybe both.

⭐ 249. Don't twist yourself into a pretzel shape to make others like you or accept you.

⭐ 250. Don't stay small in any relationship or area of your life to please someone else. Thrive! Burst forth!

251. No matter what the other person does, keep taking care of yourself.

252. Keep yourself safe.

253. "Save some love for me." That is a mantra for you to tell yourself. Don't give all of your self-love to someone else.

254. Trust the process enough to let go.

255. You deserve to live a life free from chaos, fear, crisis, rage, resentment and self-pity.

256. Actions speak louder than words.

257. Listen to the lyrics of the song Both Sides Now by Joni Mitchell. Might give you a little insight into part of your life.

258. Do not be in a relationship for the wrong reasons.

259. Do you have some inner stuff that you need to work out?

260. No experience is a failure. Every experience has a silver lining. Even things that appear negative have a gift within.

261. Close your eyes. Think about this question. Do you feel loved and connected in your relationship? Is your partner as "involved" in your relationship as you are? Is he

stable?

⭐ 262. Take care of yourself and let others take care of themselves.

⭐ 263. Don't isolate when you are in pain. Share your feelings with a trusted friend.

⭐ 264. Do you know what some say EGO means? Edging God Out.

265. Do you feel that you have gotten a Master's Degree in Relationships with all of the lessons that you have learned?

266. Do you want a sense of calm in your life? Listen to your heart. Listen to your head. Do you feel dread and anxiety when you have conversations about relationship issues? After the conversations, do you feel confused, attacked, threatened, or mistrusting? You do know what you need to do.

267. Leave a relationship that is filled with loud, angry, hostile words, and actions. You want to be with someone who reacts and interacts in a healthy, adult way.

268. It is hard to let go emotionally even when you know he is not good for you.

269. "I can see clearly now. I can choose not to suffer."

270. Ask God to give you a reality check. The message will come!

271. Feel your feelings. Express them honestly to your pillow. Say everything that you want to say to the person that you are not able to talk to. Vent. Get it all out. Cry. Scream.

272. Maybe this relationship feels like a mistake. Mistakes are opportunities to learn.

273. If I believe that your journey is going the wrong way, I do not have to travel that path with you. I have a right to believe in the merit of my beliefs. (You are leaving the relationship because of someone's behavior.)

274. You need to detach physically and emotionally so that you can experience relief from anguish, confusion, and misery.

275. Stop feeling sorry for yourself. If you do what you have always done, you will get what you have always gotten. It is time to shake things up and do things differently.

276. I cannot force another person to love me, call me, come to visit me, care about me, think like I do, stay with me, go out of his way for me or feel like I do about things.

277. Has he ever just driven away in anger? Left your house without

saying goodbye? Glared at you with an anger in his eyes that frightened you?

278. You may feel like you are taking two steps forward and one step back when you are making changes in a relationship pattern. Hang on. You know what is right and what is wrong. You know what was unacceptable to you in the relationship. Now that you have the awareness, you have to take the action that is best for you. Things will get better. Healing from a

relationship takes time. Give God time.

★ 279. Are you disillusioned? Have you experienced more than what you know is right in terms of tears, hurt and heartache?

★ 280. Face reality.

★ 281. Write it all out. Express all of your feelings. Hide your journal really well or toss the pages away. The writing is just a way for you to express yourself in a safe way.

⭐ 282. Leave a person who often blames you or is angry with you.

⭐ 283. Take a drive. Find a quiet place to sit and think. Listen to the birds chirping. Watch the sun rise or set. Experience peace and quiet for a few hours. You will probably have a realization of what is going on with your partner. "Ah-ha, I get it now." The solution, answer or inspiration will come.

284. You may feel wobbly emotionally when you are at the starting point. You are learning what you are supposed to learn. A valuable change is going to take place.

285. Are you going to worry about what the future may bring? Or live and appreciate the moments that you have right now.

286. If you are listening in on someone's phone conversations or spying on them because you think that there is

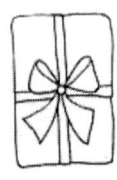    

something "fishy" going on, I'll bet you are right.

⭐ 287. Everything in life is "temporary."

⭐ 288. Do I know what is best for me? Yes! And I know what is wrong too.

⭐ 289. Remember the feelings of being angry, betrayed and distraught? Do you want to live the rest of your life being exposed to those negative feelings? Get out while you can.

290. Repeat as often as necessary. You don't matter anymore to me. You don't matter anymore to me.

291. You may hear a song and it will remind you of something pleasant about the relationship. You may feel nostalgic for the happy and joyful times. Don't go backwards. Do not call, text or email. You know the hurts and the unmet needs in your relationship. If you have decided that you are moving forward, be strong. Take out your "Ouch List" where

you have recorded all of the things that were mixed-up, unhealthy, tense, and unacceptable, out of bounds, depressing, bad, and crazy, boggled your mind, tragic, sad, dangerous or evil. Talk, cry and laugh. Remember the good times but most importantly, REALLY remember why you are saying Goodbye. Use your gifts of serenity, wisdom and courage.

292. Awareness, Acceptance and Action. Putting them together is the formula

for recovering from the confusion and pain.

293. Face the truth. You know the truth. Don't deny the plain truth. You know your deep dark thoughts.

294. There is no "one size fits all" method of saying Goodbye to a relationship that is not good for you. Your partner may think everything is fine. Respect yourself. Speak your truth. Make the choice that is best for

your life. Don't accept unacceptable behavior. Be kind to yourself.

295. "That tone of voice is unacceptable." You are allowed to stand up for yourself.

296. God, please guide me with whatever I am supposed to learn from this relationship.

297. Do not ask a man a question unless you are prepared to hear his answer. Prepare to hear him answer

honestly. You may not like what he has to say to you. It is not necessarily true. You just want to listen.

298. You know what a good relationship is like. You have been in relationships where the man would go to the end of the earth to help you. A person who loves to be with you. How does this guy compare to other men that have liked you?

299. I feel bad that I have been with him and let this happen to me. What was I thinking? Why didn't I realize what was happening?

300. Have you found yourself crying at night? Obsessing about a problem?

301. There comes a time that you realize that ranting, explaining, exploding, preaching and losing your temper with your partner is not going to change the person, situation, addiction, habit

or whatever else is just not working for you. You are not his therapist!

302. There is a God who knows vastly more than you do about the relationship that is best for you. Not all relationships are as difficult as the one that you are involved in.

303. "You just don't understand." Are you tired of saying that or feeling that?

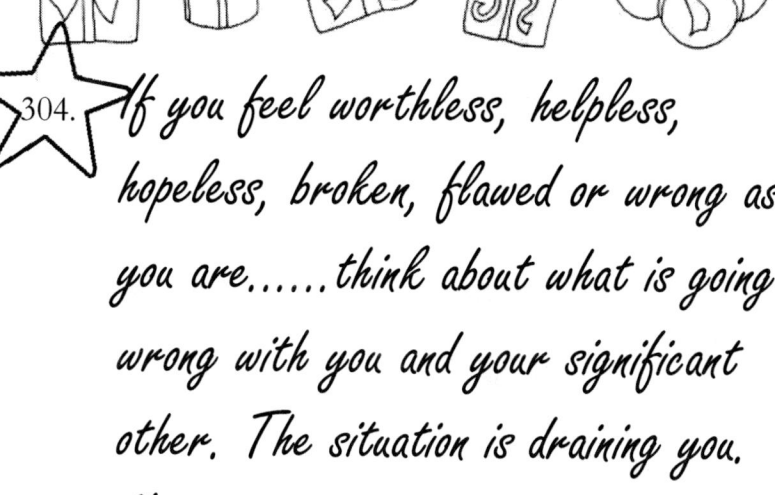

304. If you feel worthless, helpless, hopeless, broken, flawed or wrong as you are......think about what is going wrong with you and your significant other. The situation is draining you. You need to revive your spirit.

305. Are you looking for a partner to make you feel happy, worthy, loved, of value? Do you think that is a realistic expectation?

306. Engrave this message on your heart and soul. That person would make my

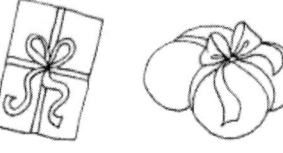

life miserable.

307. When you have made the decision that the relationship is over - that it is no longer working for you then tell yourself: I can have no further contact with the person. We cannot be friends. We cannot get together to talk anymore. It has all been said. I need to be strong. I know that this relationship would not enhance my life. I still care. No doubt, I still see the good in this person. I still have memories of the good times. I am doing this because I care about me.

Don't take the risk and go back. If you know what you know, give yourself the Gift of Resolve.

308. Listen to the song "I Can See Clearly Now" – some of the lyrics may apply to your situation.

309. Rejection is protection.

310. Ask God to help you focus on what is important – today – and then manage your life one day at a time.

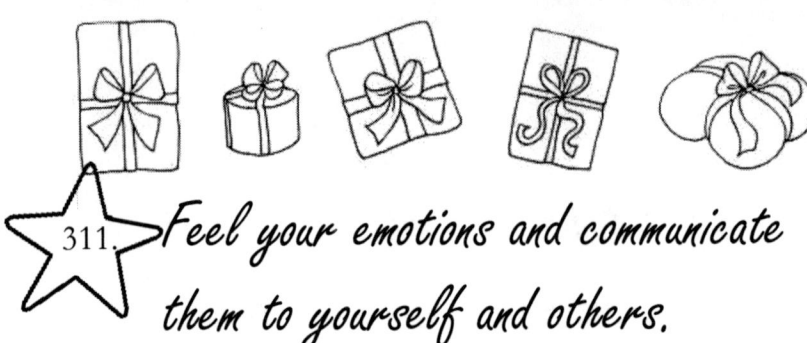

311. Feel your emotions and communicate them to yourself and others.

312. Fill your days with new experiences and personal growth.

313. Loving yourself is a gift that keeps on growing – and keeps you going!

314. Be responsible for yourself and let others be responsible for themselves.

315. I am worth it. I am giving myself a huge gift - The Courageous and Self-Respecting Gift of Saying Goodbye.

316. Treat yourself to something special today. You deserve it.

317. Learn new things. Kayaking, Contra dancing, computer skills, a new language, white water rafting, skiing, ice skating, etc.

318. Maybe this is an experience where God took over for you. He knew that this relationship was not in His plan for you.

319. The only person that you can change is yourself. How you feel about yourself will determine how you will react in any given situation.

320. Get your groove back. Get your hopes and dreams back.

⭐ 321. Don't get into unwinnable arguments.

⭐ 322. Don't negate your feelings.

⭐ 323. Complete honesty. You deserve that. Yes, COMPLETE honesty.

⭐ 324. Do you sometimes wonder — "What was exactly wrong in the relationship?"

⭐ 325. Begin a Time for Healing.

326. Do you feel drained from trying to explain your feelings?

327. What lies ahead? I don't know but God knows.

328. You made the right decision. Say Goodbye to sadness, anxiety, despair, and hopelessness. Yes, you had good times together. Your heart, body and soul need peace and tranquility now. You have been through a lot. Map out plans for a new life.

⭐ 329. You deserve to not be in the presence of someone who is dangerously unpredictable. You have a choice to stay in a relationship or leave.

⭐ 330. It is not your job to punish someone for what they did to you. It is your job to walk away when you get to the point that enough is enough.

⭐ 331. The wisdom within you has given you insight. You have the courage within you to say Goodbye. You have to keep reminding yourself that no

further contact is the best way for you not to be drawn back into an unhealthy relationship. You may feel lonely and worry that you will never find anyone to love you again. Or that maybe you over-reacted to unacceptable behavior. Don't doubt yourself. There was a whole long list of things that were not right in the relationship. If you went back, it would be more of the same.

332. Denial is a great defense. Were you angry sometimes and took it out on

yourself? Overeating, nervous habits, trouble sleeping? Have you taken medication to relieve the anxiety that you felt about the relationship?

333. Do the right thing for yourself.

334. Let go of the things that you have no control over.

335. Waiting for another person to change is not how it works. The change

needs to be within me. I can change no one but myself.

336. All relationships are not meant to last a lifetime.

337. Sometimes people come into your life exactly when you need them and they leave when God determines that you no longer need them. Trust that something else will appear that is for your highest good. His time, not mine.

338. Be honest – could your present relationship ruin your future?

339. God, it's your day. Let it be your way. Let me know if I should stay or go away.

340. There comes a time when you recognize that you can no longer ignore what is happening in the relationship.

341. Is the relationship a disaster? Spiritually, emotionally, or physically.

342. Leaving a relationship is not an admission of guilt or failure. It is a confirmation of your strength and courage. Your decision is a wise one – you are not going to put up with bad behavior, thoughtlessness, disrespect or selfishness.

☆ 343. Are you worrying about something night after night? Are you refusing to see the truth about something?

☆ 344. Have you ever feared that he was involved in something illegal or criminal?

☆ 345. Has he called and cancelled plans at the last minute?

☆ 346. Are you desperate to be heard and understood by your partner? What if

there is an irreconcilable difference?

⭐ 347. *You know what you want. Go for it. Move forward. Don't fall down into the abyss.*

⭐ 348. *Have you ever sat down and had an honest discussion with him and asked him to tell you how he really feels about you? Sit still, listen, do not respond or show emotion. Let him speak. Do not interrupt. Accept what he says as his opinion.*

349. Acceptance is allowing God to do what I cannot do.

350. The path to peace is accepting people, places and things as they are.

351. I have to matter to me first! You get to choose who you will give your heart to. Not whether he wants you. That is backwards. You are the gold. You decide who is worth giving yourself to.

⭐ 352. Sometimes, we get what we give. Give gratitude, appreciation, love, etc. It may have the boomerang effect.

⭐ 353. I accept that I am utterly powerless over what someone else is thinking, doing or going to do. You cannot monitor another person, no matter how well-meaning your intentions are.

⭐ 354. Why would you want to be with someone that you have to check up on

or monitor? Chances are you are right about what you are worried about anyway.

⭐ 355. You now probably know the unmanageable things in your partner's life.

⭐ 356. You can only fix the unmanageable things in your life.

⭐ 357. Be careful - beware of who you fall in love with.

358. Have you noticed a tendency towards explosive behavior, moodiness, and road rage, poor relationships with his family members, threatening, blaming or intimidating behavior?

359. Now that you think about it, is the person capable of fidelity with a partner?

360. Has the person blamed you or projected things that are shortcomings for him upon you? Does he have a tendency to twist the

conversation around so that whatever you say to him bounces back negatively upon you?

361. Every once in a while, you see hope that the relationship might be working well. Then something happens. You see deviant or inappropriate behavior.

362. Sometimes it is hard to know the difference between a true crisis and your own tendency to blow things out of proportion. Ask God what is going

on. And listen to what He tells you is the next right step.

⭐ 363 Something may happen that makes you upset. Maybe God is giving you a message. I didn't listen. God nudged me. And then God spoke louder. It was then that I knew that I was going to give myself The Courageous and Self-Respecting Gift of Saying Goodbye.

⭐ 364 The only person I need to control is me. It is too much work and only an

illusion that you can control anyone else.

365. When you feel shame or embarrassment for your actions in a relationship that is a sign that things are in need of a tune-up.

366. I am ending this relationship now. I don't know the outcome of this decision but I trust my inner guide. I can count on the loving beneficence of God to help me through this unknown situation.

367. My loss of serenity is making me feel upset. Now that I am aware of how someone else's behavior has affected me, I can accept life on life's terms. I accept the fact that now that I am aware, I can take action. Action that will restore me to balance and serenity in my life.

368. You have the freedom to end a relationship.

369. Accept the things you cannot change and move on out of the relationship.

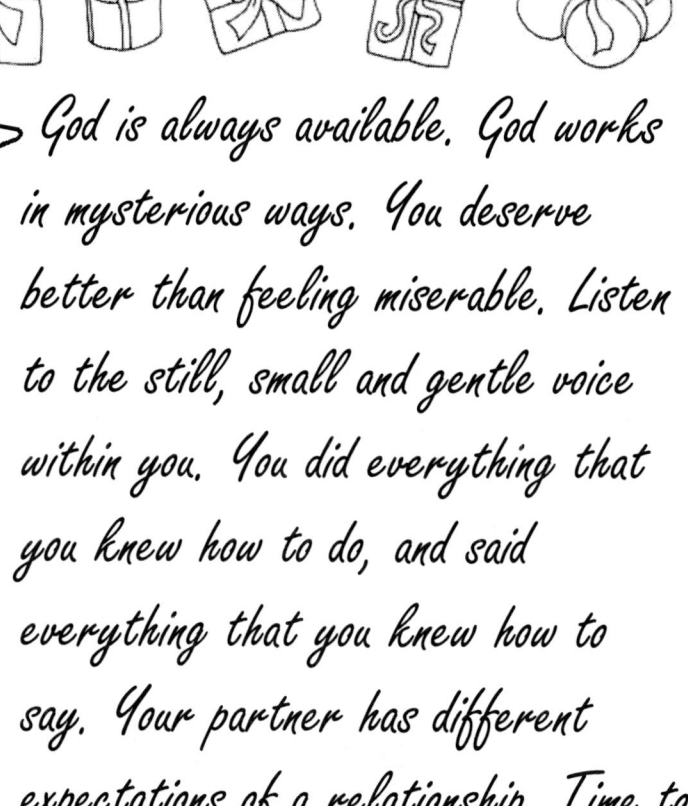

370. God is always available. God works in mysterious ways. You deserve better than feeling miserable. Listen to the still, small and gentle voice within you. You did everything that you knew how to do, and said everything that you knew how to say. Your partner has different expectations of a relationship. Time to exit and find peace.

371. Have the courage to change the things that you can.

372. *You have the wisdom to know the difference between what you can and should accept. You also have the courage to know that things are not going well and it is time to move on out of the relationship.*

373. *No relationship is ideal. But if your friends and family were aware of some of the things going on in your relationship, they would tell you to get out now.*

374. Learn to take care of yourself in a relationship. Are you tired of the darned aggravation? Obsessing? Wondering? Feeling bad or sad?

375. Unclutter your mind. Unclutter your life. It is not a failure to leave the romantic relationship. It is a lesson.

376. Is he a "street angel" and "house devil?"

⭐ 377. What would you tell your daughter if she was in a relationship like yours?

⭐ 378. After you have prayed the prayer: "Lord, please don't let me stay in this relationship one second more than I am supposed to" - keep listening for a message.

⭐ 379. You may have to pray that prayer for several weeks. Little things will show up. Things that you know are unhealthy for you. Perhaps,

emotionally abusive. They wound you, hurt you and upset you. Heed the message.

380. Get up. Get out. Get going.

381. You might feel bad that you did not see it all. You missed cues and clues. Don't be hard on yourself. Guys like this know what they are doing. A nice woman like you can be conned in this way. You are not naïve. You have been around the block a few times. You are intelligent, kind and

caring. This guy did not deserve you. He hurt your feelings. He took your trust. It will take you some time to heal. Because before you discovered what he was really all about, you thought he was a good man. He wasn't all bad. He had "issues" – or maybe an addiction that you do not have to put up with.

382. Detach. Leave. Get off the crazy train. Disembark. Run for your life! He would make your life miserable.

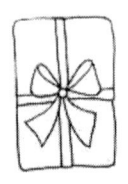    

⭐ 383. I challenge you to get a big piece of paper. I bet you can write 74 things that bothered you about this relationship. Ready, get set, go!

⭐ 384. The stages of grief after a loss may take you through these stages: denial, anger, bargaining, depression, and acceptance. You may experience them in any order and they may occur over and over again.

⭐ 385. You may experience numbness emotionally and feel unbalanced and

disorganized. You may feel intense emotional suffering.

386. Knowing you are going to break up with someone may take you to the stage of "anticipatory sadness."

387. "What if he tells his friends about something in our relationship, what if he gets back at me and slanders my good name, what will other people think about me if he makes things up about me?" There is nothing that you can do about that. Stay away from

him. Have no more contact – none at all.

⭐ 388 You have to forgive yourself! For what? You might be wondering how I could have been so dumb, stupid, idiotic or naive to have stayed in a relationship with him. (These are not my words but the words many women who come to counseling sessions with me use.) "I saw signs that were a little troublesome but I thought maybe he didn't mean it that way, maybe I am just not used to dating,

maybe I am reading too much into it, maybe he did not really do that, maybe I am analyzing this too much, or maybe I should overlook this because nobody is perfect." You might be feeling bad about yourself, for staying longer than you think that you should have. But in reality, you stayed "exactly" how much time that you needed to – to realize what was really going on – what was really happening. It took that long for you to discover his true colors. And when that moment of clarity came, you

knew that you had to make a decision. A very tough one.

⭐ 389. You will wonder about him. You will think about him. It may take a long time for you to move on. You have been wounded, scarred and changed by this relationship.

⭐ 390. Throw his pictures away. Burn his letters and cards. Trash his emails. Block his calls and texts.

⭐ 391. Nothing changes if nothing changes.

⭐ 392. Don't dial up pain. (Don't call the troublemakers in your life.)

⭐ 393. I can't. God can. I need to let Him.

⭐ 394. When the mother gets healthy, the family gets better.

★ 395. Help someone: say YOUR prayers - Bless them. Help me. Help them. Bless me.

★ 396. You are very important. (Post on your mirror for daily reading.)

★ 397. I am worth the changes that are good for me.

★ 398. When one person over-functions, the other under-functions.

⭐ 399. I am doing this because I care about me.

⭐ 400. NO is a complete sentence. Stop explaining yourself to others.

⭐ 401. Mind your own business. (When helping too much hurts them, let go and let God help them.)

⭐ 402. The importance of wearing an I LOVE MYSELF BRACELET. My daughter bought a bracelet for me

and one for herself in 2001. "When we wear this bracelet, Mom, it is to remind us that we need to take care of ourselves first before we can help someone else. We have to love ourselves."

COACHING SERVICES

PAY BY THE MINUTE CONSULTATION WITH AUTHOR PATRICIA GALLAGHER.

As support to the many people who are struggling to understand their relationship and personal issues, I offer life coaching by telephone, or in-person at my office in a Philadelphia suburb. At $1.00 per minute through PayPal, my clients are able to choose how much of my time that they feel they need.

If you would like to speak with me, contact me to arrange an appointment. I'll call you, so you won't have any long distance phone charges.

Patricia Gallagher BA, MBA
Phone: 267-939-0365
www.patriciausa.com
Box 561, Worcester, PA 19490

TO EVERYTHING THERE IS A SEASON

To everything there is a season, and a time to every purpose under the heaven:

A time to be born, and a time to die; a time to plant, and a time to pluck up that which is planted;

A time to kill, and a time to heal; a time to break down, and a time to build up;

A time to weep, and a time to laugh; a time to mourn, and a time to dance;

A time to cast away stones, and a time to gather stones together; a time to embrace, and a time to refrain from embracing;

A time to get, and a time to lose; a time to keep, and a time to cast away;

A time to rend, and a time to sew; a time to keep silence, and a time to speak;

A time to love, and a time to hate; a time of war, and a time of peace.

What profit hath he that worketh in that wherein he laboureth?
I have seen the travail, which God hath given to the sons of men to be exercised in it.
He hath made everything beautiful in his time: also he hath set the world in his heart, so that no man can find out the work that God maketh from the beginning to the end.
I know that there is no good in them, but for a man to rejoice, and to do good in his life.

(Book of Ecclesiastes)

For more information about books, workshops and presentations:

Patricia Gallagher
Box 561
Worcester, PA 19490
Telephone: (267) 939 0365
www.patriciausa.com

Patricia Gallagher's books are available at special quantity discounts for bulk purchases for sales promotions, premiums, book discussion groups, or fund-raising. Contact the author for special sales orders. Books also available on Kindle and Amazon.

Bring Patricia Gallagher to your church or organization. She is available for:
- Seminars on a variety of topics
- Training for small group leaders
- Conferences
- Educational events
- Consulting with individuals/organizations

If you are interested in visiting Patricia Gallagher at her counseling center, please call (267) 939-0365. Suburb of Philadelphia.

QUESTIONS FOR BOOK DISCUSSION GROUP

- How did the author's voice or opinions shape your understanding of this subject?
- How did this book change your views on the subject matter it presented?
- Are your opinions different now than they were before reading the book?
- What made this book different than other books on this subject?
- Do you think it is better or worse than other books on this subject matter?
- Read your favorite passage from the book out loud.
- Explain why you liked it or what it made you think about.
- What else can you add to the discussion about this topic?
- What are some possible lessons from this book?
- What was memorable about this book?

ABOUT THE AUTHOR

Patricia Gallagher is the author of fourteen books. She has appeared as a guest on the following shows: *Oprah Winfrey, Sally Jessy Raphael, The CBS Early Show, Maury Povich, QVC, The 700 Club, CNN, CNBC, Financial News Network, Interview with Joan Lunden*, and hundreds of other interview shows. She was contacted by the *Dr. Phil Show* and *People Magazine* for her most recent book, *No More Secrets – A Family Speaks about Depression, Anxiety, and Attempted Suicide*. She has appeared more than once on most of the above shows.

She holds a BA in Education from Villanova University and an MBA in

Finance from Saint Joseph's University. She has been a media consultant/product spokesperson for Holiday Inn, Resolve Carpet Cleaner, Off! Skintastic Insect Repellant, Stouffer's Frozen Lasagna, Lysol Disinfectant Spray, Johnson & Johnson RED CROSS® Brand All-Purpose First Aid Kit, Environments' Educational Supplies, the Scotsman's Group, the Diaper Manufacturers of America, Eastwind Airlines, and others.

She has worked with leading global public relations and communications firms such as Ruder–Finn, Burson-Marsteller and the Product Spokesperson Network.

Features and reviews about Patricia's books have been in print publications such as: *Family Circle, The Wall Street Journal, Woman's World, Parents Magazine, the Stars and Stripes* military newspaper and others.

Her books and Team of Angels Project have been featured in media news services such as Gannett, UPI, Associated Press, and Scripps Howard.

Patricia created the *Send a Team of Angels to Help Movement* which has distributed over 100,000 Team of Angels pins worldwide. The mission is to spread, hope and comfort, one angel pin at a time!

She is currently the Director of the Happy Flower Day Project. The mission is to spread love and joy to seniors in nursing homes, assisted living facilities and anywhere else by bringing beautiful bouquets of flowers donated by Trader Joe's.

She is the mother of four and the grandmother of one, and lives in a suburb of Philadelphia.

For more information about Patricia Gallagher's books, consultations, workshops or presentations:

Patricia Gallagher
Box 561
Worcester, PA 19490
Telephone: (267) 939 0365
www.patriciausa.com

LETTERS FROM WOMEN WHO LEARNED THINGS ABOUT THEMSELVES WHEN THEY SAID GOODBYE

After a counseling session with Jean, I challenged her to go home and write her feelings down about why her relationship felt so difficult, why she felt rejected so often, why they fought so much, etc. I suggested that we meet again the following week. Two months passed by. I thought that she had not made any changes in her life. Jean had made some important decisions during that period. Here are her reflections about The Courageous and Self-Respecting Gift of Saying Goodbye. She gave me permission to share this with the readers of this book.

Dear Patricia,

    I have six favorite friends - ones who understand me. The ones who understood for almost a year that at past middle age it felt nice for me to be in a happy romantic relationship - where I felt loved and appreciated. They understood why I needed to be held when I felt sad. And comforted when my daughter's drug addiction became too much for me to handle alone. When I needed someone to be with me as I went through the heartache of moving out of my family home and made the decision to move in with him.

    At the same time, I was caring for my father and went through the triple whammy of losing my job, dealing with a father with Alzheimer's, and grieving the estrangement from my only adult child. Tom was the man who came into my life to help me. Hurt me. Confuse me. Take my trust. And teach me a lesson. Tonight rain poured down. Beads of rain pelted the windows. I felt lonely, sad, hurt and angry. I yearned for the things that we had for the better part of a year. The nice dinners, the rides to the mountains, attending church services, Oldies dances, outdoor concerts; someone who listened so well, cared about me and my family. And much more. But tonight I really "got" it.

Enough stomachaches, headaches, biting my lip nervously. Enough uncertainty. Enough wondering about honesty, lies of omission, fidelity, drinking and morality.

I did not have to refer to my list of the things that were not right in our relationship. The computer file bulged with the notes that I typed each time that he said or did something that did not make sense to me. (Or I could not possibly understand.) I knew them by heart now. And there were scads of them. Five weeks have passed since we have been together. Four weeks since we last spoke by phone. Three weeks since I stopped answering emails or texts.

I told myself that I would not respond to him ever again. I prayed for the resolve to mean what I said. In my private conversations with my pillow, I told Tom that I hated him. And I told him I liked him too. In my middle of the night conversations. He never heard the conversations. Just between me and my wet pillow. And when the three emails/texts arrived this week, I wanted to do something. But didn't.

I thought of self-respect, self-love and self-care. I thought of what I would tell my daughter if she shared the same circumstance in her relationships. I knew the answer without hesitation. Tonight, I feel strong. Courageous. Certain. As I cleaned my room – folded clothes, hung scarves and untangled jewelry, I untangled my thoughts. The clock hands ticked at 3:51 am.

"Why didn't I walk away at the first red flag?"

I still had things to learn. I did not know what was going on. I learned the scorching truth by walking through the fire. Taught me and changed me. Like no other relationship in my life. I often prayed at times of frustration.

"God, please do not let me stay in this relationship one second more than I am supposed to. Please let me see what you want me to see, hear what you want me to hear and know what you want me to know."

And bits of information appeared. I added each new thing to my list.

I know what I know. I need my heart to tell my head what I know. I know what I know. (The words repeated over and over in my subconscious mind.)

And all of the pieces of the past few months that did not make sense fell into place. Between the hours of midnight and 3:51 am. Between sorting shoes and hanging up pocketbooks.

As I untangled the necklaces, I found the inner strength to let go of Tom. The man who caused havoc with my emotions. Havoc a few days here and there. Havoc that added up to weeks, months and almost a year of confusion.

Let go. Let him go, Jeannie. If God wanted him in your life, he would be here now. As the hands on the clock moved to 3:56 am, my heart and my head knew that I must make him mean nothing to me anymore. God clearly showed me the issues tonight. My prayers have been answered.

He was never the man that I thought he was. Tom showed me who he was - over and over. *When someone tells you who he is – believe him – the first time.* I would never have dated him if I had known these things.

As I cleaned my room, I saw things as if I were wearing a clean pair of glasses. And I saw the gift. The gift of him coming into my life for a reason and a season. And the gift of me leaving. And the gift of him leaving my sacred personal holy space – with my self-respect intact.

Feeling deceived, betrayed and violated by all that I did not know about his morals, integrity and character. Tom did not meet my standards. The relationship was not easy. It was time to get off the crazy train.

"Thank you, God, for giving me the courage to leave a destructive relationship." Tonight I prayed for a spiritual decision. To accept the blessed lesson given to me - the lesson in self-respect. I have a gift to share with the next woman walking this path.

I had the gift of an exciting and joyful relationship most of the time. But the gift was very costly. And the price to stay in that relationship would bankrupt my spirit and life.

I have the gift of saying Goodbye. Not to him personally. I know that No Further Contact ever is still the right path for me. I asked myself, "What are the words that describe how you feel?" *Violated, deceived, betrayed, and cheated upon.*

I'll just tell my pillow and God in my private conversation tonight. *Thank you for giving me the ability to let go of a man and a situation that proved unhealthy for me.*

I know what I know. I know what I know. I know what I know. I must trust what I know. And what I knew was true. Thank you, Patricia, for guiding me through this major transition in my life. Gratefully yours,
Jeannie

Dear Patricia,

I did what you suggested. First, I told myself that he is not a bad person. He is just a bad person for me. Then, I got rid of the things that reminded me of him. I had a big black suitcase that contained the clothes that I had worn on our trip to Minnesota. Every outfit was a "reminder" - the dress I wore when I went to visit his mother, the pants suit that I wore when we went to the concert, and the pink pajamas that I wore when we stayed at the Dude Ranch along our travels. I loaded the suitcase into the front seat of my car and took it to a big green dumpster. I threw it in. Crash. Bang. I heard the automatic "crusher" in the community dumpster smash it to smithereens! I guess that was symbolic in a way for me to do that. I couldn't look at those clothes without a memory attached. I needed to detach from the clothes and from the relationship. I am so glad that I heard your presentation. I am ready to move forward in my life.
Laura

Dear Patricia,

Baby steps first, right? I turned his picture upside down on my bureau. I told you that I just could not throw it away. That is, until I knew that it was not helping me to look at it every morning. One day, I just told myself, "Joanie, just do it." And I did. No more picture. Some people can have reminders but for me, I know that the best thing is to put that chapter behind me. And if that means, I had to throw a perfectly nice picture away, so be it.
Joan

Dear Patricia,

   I am tempted to go back to the places where we spent time together. To the dances and his church, to the outdoor concerts that he frequents and to the places we went to when we were a couple. To the Beef 'n Beer restaurant where we met. I know that if I did, that I would see his friends there or maybe even him. I am not strong enough to resist the temptation to start things up again. You told me NO MORE CONTACT. So, I am making a promise to you, to not go where I might "just bump into him accidentally." He is related to my brother-in-law so it is a tough situation.
Sarah

Dear Patricia,

You told me that it would be hard. Hard to really put this relationship behind me. I still talk to my friends about him and "analyze" all of the details of the breakup. It is just that despite all of the negative things that happened, there were good times too. I will just keep the "snapshot" in my mind of the time that he hurt me and I know that is what finally ended it all. There is no excusing that act of anger towards me. And honestly, that was not the only time that I saw unacceptable things happen in our relationship. I did not trust him when he went out with his best friend. I am not going back.
Mary Lou

Dear Patricia,

    He has a best friend. A single guy - well, they have both been married three times but they still believe in going out together drinking and being merry. Much more merry – in my opinion - than grown men should be doing. They think they are teenagers. I just don't like some of the things they are involved in such as going to "raunchy movies." I think they say "Birds of a feather flock together." You told me that I have to be as wise as a serpent and gentle as a lamb. I think you said that was from the Bible. I wrote him a letter saying all that I was feeling. Not in anger. Just my true feelings. I had shown him my anger earlier in the week so he knew where I stood on the issues. I am releasing him from my world. My kind of man does not need to go to "inappropriate" locales. Thank you for guiding me.
Evelyn

OTHER BOOKS BY PATRICIA C. GALLAGHER

AS SEEN ON THE OPRAH SHOW THREE TIMES

Home Child Care

How to Set Up a Fun and Successful Day Care Business in Your Own Home

Patricia C. Gallagher BA, MBA

Patricia Gallagher's Books Are Available on Amazon and Kindle.

Patricia Gallagher's Books Are Available on Amazon and Kindle.

Patricia Gallagher's Books Are Available on Amazon and Kindle.

AS SEEN ON THE OPRAH SHOW THREE TIMES

THE GIFT OF BELIEVING IN YOURSELF

Spirit-Lifting Thoughts for Each Day

Patricia C. Gallagher BA, MBA

Patricia Gallagher's Books Are Available on Amazon and Kindle.

The Gift of Changing Yourself

Daily Reflections for Women in Transition

Patricia C. Gallagher BA, MBA

AS SEEN ON THE OPRAH SHOW THREE TIMES

Patricia Gallagher's Books Are Available on Amazon and Kindle.

Patricia Gallagher's Books Are Available on Amazon and Kindle.

Patricia Gallagher's Books Are Available on Amazon and Kindle.

Patricia Gallagher's Books Are Available on Amazon and Kindle.

Patricia Gallagher's Books Are Available on Amazon and Kindle.

Patricia Gallagher's Books Are Available on Amazon and Kindle.

AS SEEN ON THE OPRAH SHOW THREE TIMES

The Courageous and Self-Respecting Gift of Saying Goodbye

For Anyone Considering Parting Ways in a Relationship and Who Needs the Strength to Let Go

Patricia Clare Gallagher BA, MBA

CPSIA information can be obtained
at www.ICGtesting.com
Printed in the USA
LVOW12s1107030117
519551LV00001B/173/P